IMAGES OF SCOTLAND

MOTHERWELL

The Moir family of Motherwell.

IMAGES OF SCOTLAND

MOTHERWELL

HELEN MOIR

This book is dedicated to my husband, Bill, and our family

First published 1999

Reprinted 2004

Reprinted in 2008 by
The History Press
The Mill, Brimscombe Port,
Stroud, Gloucestershire, GL5 2QG
www.thehistorypress.co.uk

Reprinted 2011

Copyright © Helen Moir, 1999

ISBN 978 0 7524 1801 8

Typesetting and origination by
Tempus Publishing Limited
Printed and bound in England.

Contents

Introduction		7
1.	A Walk Around Motherwell	13
2.	A Night at the Cinema	43
3.	Transport	47
4.	Haulage	57
5.	Industry	61
6.	Churches	71
7.	Do You Recognize Anyone?	77
8.	Football	95
9.	Another Walk Around Motherwell	101

Acknowledgements

I would like to give a very special thank you to the following people and institutions: Kenny Clark, Richard Devanney, George Dingwall, Jim Fyfe (Carfin Grotto), Charles McBain, Matt McCluckie, Scott McCutcheon, J.J. McKillop, Peter Moir Jnr, Mrs Morton, James Muncie, Ronnie Porteous, Tom Shaw, Tom Sneddon, Jane Sykes, Motherwell Bridge, Motherwell Heritage Centre (Brian Kirk and Margaret McGarry), and St Mary's church. This book could not have been accomplished without their help and donations of their precious material.

I would also like to thank Ian Skelly for his marvellous support and his belief in me and my material.

Special thanks to Gina Moir for her marvellous help and a special mention to Billy, Sam, Adam, Elaine, James, Gina, Amanda, Jason, William and Nicole.

Introduction

The town of Motherwell lies about twelve miles south-east of Glasgow and has been one of the principal towns of Lanarkshire since the mid nineteenth century. The town is situated in what was the Parish of Dalziel and although the history of the modern town of Motherwell as we perceive it today is comparatively young, the history of the parish is much older and, indeed, the name Motherwell has possibly been derived from a number of other off shoots.

A number of theories have been presented for the origin of the name Motherwell and I shall now list a few of them. The name 'Modyrval' appears in the thirteenth century and seemingly has a religious connection with the lands of Modyrval belonging to the monks of Paisley Abbey. The Abbey holds records that refer to 'Modiryal'. Other spellings are 'Mod ryall', 'Modrall', 'Modyrwall', 'Modervale', 'Moderville', 'Moderwiell' and 'Modruell'. David II of Scotland, son of King Robert the Bruce and his second wife Elizabeth, granted a charter in the fourteenth century in which the name of the lands appears as 'Modyrwaile'.

The name 'Motherwell' as we know it in its present format did not come into use until the eighteenth century. A theory put forward is that the name comes from the old English word 'Wael', meaning pool or well. At one point in history this well was dedicated to Mary the mother of Jesus (The Mother Well), and hence the connection. This theory has come under some intense scrutiny by folk who say that the name mother in Scotland was not commonly used when one was referring to the 'Virgin Mary' and that the name Lady would have been the more obvious choice. She is often referred to by some as 'Our Lady'. There is an area in Motherwell known as Ladywell where a well did once exist. Another theory is that it has Celtic origin with 'Moi' or 'Mo' meaning a level place and 'Hyl' meaning 'the level place above a river'

Motherwell has two rivers running near the town – the famous River Clyde and the Calder. The River Clyde runs to the west of the town and the River Calder to the north. In the 1816 map produced by William Forrest, Motherwell Village is marked along with north and south Motherwell and Ladywell.

Motherwell, like a lot of other Scottish towns, was formed through small clusters of dwellings and hamlets beginning to link up, caused by population growth, work capacity and just sheer expansion. In the 1816 map, names such as Windmillhill, Milton. Coursington, Jerviston and Carfin also appeared, and from these small dwellings the nucleus of Motherwell was formed. These dwellings all lived under the auspices of the Dalzell Hamiltons, whose seat was at Dalziel House, reminiscent of so many other parts of Scotland.

Whatever the origin of the name, to her inhabitants she is loved and held dearly. Though the town is comparatively young, the Barony of Dalziel goes back to ninth-century Scotland and the recorded history of the area goes back to the second century AD, when the Roman conquerors invaded our lands. A Roman road cuts right through the Dalziel Parish in John Ainslie's map of 1789 and is clearly marked. It is also noted in General Roy's map of 1747.

Archaeological digs in the area have given us a great insight into Roan life in Scotland. The Romans brought, compared to our native Britons of this area, a very enlightened and forward thinking culture, even if their methods of conquest were somewhat barbaric. The digs have included a Roman fort being excavated at Bothwellhaugh, lying halfway between Motherwell and Bellshill, during 1967-1987, and later, in 1975-1976, the discovery of a bath. A fine example of Roman architecture is to be seen at the Roman Bridge. The bridge crosses over the Calder, thus joining the two parishes of Dalziel and Bothwell. A more modern legend is attached to the ancient bridge. The legend goes that the ill-fated Mary Queen of Scots moored her boat to an iron ring, still visible, while on her visit to Orbiston.

The Romans gave the name 'Strathclyde' to the region, with 'Strath' meaning valley. Camp Road in Motherwell is a reminder to its folk of their connection to the mighty Roman Empire.

The next force that arrived was to become, and still is, very much part of Scotland's story – Christianity. The earliest religious building in Motherwell was St Patrick's church of Dalziel, dedicated to the well-known St Patrick, dismantled in 1798. The place then became the site for Lord Hamilton's Mausoleum. The order of the monk was later to see the building of some of the most beautiful and ornate monasteries. The monk, although leading what was really a secular life, played a large part in stabilizing the countryside, seeing to the spiritual needs of their flock while working the land. Pagan Scotland was no more and Christianity had won the day.

The family of Dalziel has a long and illustrious pedigree, which goes back to Kenneth MacAlpin of Scotland in the ninth century. In 1343, Sir Robert Dalzell unfortunately lost the Barony of Dalzell for daring to reside in England without the consent of his king, David II of Scotland, son of the famous Robert the Bruce. The Barony was restored to the family in 1395, however, changing the state crown and political scene in Scotland. Charles I elevated Sir Robert Dalzell to the head of the family in 1628, giving him the title of Lord Dalzell, later adding Earl of Carnwath to his title in 1639. Lord Robert Dalzell moved to Carnwath, and through his nephew James Hamilton of Boggs gained the lands of Dalzell.

While doing research, I have come across two different spellings, 'Dalzell' and 'Dalziel', which can be most confusing. The explanation I have been given is that the name 'Dalziel' is connected with the name of the parish. The other spelling, 'Dalzell', seems to be connected with the estate, that is, the family, really the Hamiltons of Dalzell. The origin of the name Dalzell or Dalziel, like so much other historical data, has been lost in the myths of time and legend. A version is that it was a battle cry 'Dal Yell', – 'I Dare'. A second version is that it comes from the Gaelic *Dal Geal*, which translated into English means beautiful meadow. A lovely thought! Personally, I can visualize the battle cry, a distant ancestor to the Dalzell family running into battle calling 'Dal Yell', but that could just be my own Celtic and Pictish background coming to the fore!

In the seventeenth century the area, like so many other parts of Scotland, was caught up in the Reformation. The Reformation was one of the most turbulent times in Scotland's bloody history and the parish of Dalziel, like so many of her immediate neighbouring parishes, was in the forefront of events.

The Dalzell Hamiltons were staunch supporters of the Covenant and the Covenanters cause, to the point that one of their kin, Robert Hamilton of Monkland, was condemned to death for what was counted as his 'rebel tendencies' in 1649. The Conventicles were being held in secret throughout Scotland, one such being held in the grounds at Dalzell House beneath a huge oak tree, which still stands in the grounds today. This was referred to as 'The Covenanters Oak.' I can visualize those dedicated men and women with their children around them, braving all to practice their faith the way they wished to, under its spreading branches.

After the succession of King William III and his wife Queen Mary, peace came to what had been a troubled Scotland with the ending of the Civil War some years earlier. The beheading of Charles I meant the country had a semblance of a democratic parliament. No longer was the monarchs' power absolute. The monarch was now answerable to his country and parliament, thus putting an end to the divine right of kings, which had been held so dear by the Stewart dynasty.

After 1690 a law was passed which meant that, thankfully, both denominations, Roman Catholic and Protestant, could go without fear or hindrance to worship in freedom, in chapel or church. The decades to follow saw both churches flourish in Motherwell.

I would like now to move on to Motherwell's more modern history and try to give information to what made the town grow to eventually become one of the most industrial towns in Scotland, earning its name of the 'Steel Town.'

Motherwell in the mid-nineteenth century was still predominantly a very agricultural area. One of the biggest produce was fruit, still very much an ongoing business. A surplus of commodities in the late eighteenth century from the Dalziel Parish, such as oatmeal, hay, butter and cheese, was helping to feed the ever-growing city of Glasgow. This worked as a two-edged sword, feeding the hungry in the city and giving the farming inhabitants of Dalziel a rewarding economy.

The first factor in the town's industrial growth was cottage weaving. Men, women and children worked in their ill-lit, humble cottages, the males usually working the handlooms and the females employed in the spinning side of this very specialized craft. The excellent work they produced was mostly sold privately and was purchased by the agents of the linen merchants from Glasgow.

By the late eighteenth century the linen and threadmaking industry had begun to be taken over by the produce of another cloth, cotton. This notable advancement enhanced a trade that had its origins in the fine needlepoint done by the Tambourers. Flax was grown locally, a long complex from a small slender root with its blue bonnet grown in the field. First it was pulled up by its root when ready, bound, and then placed in at trench with constant running water. This was called 'Retting'. Then it was dried and sent to be heckled or scutched, the last process leaving the finer strands ready for weaving into cloth. The 'Hecklers Row', once situated near Motherwell Cross, was a row of one-storey houses originally inhabited by flax dressers, then cotton weavers and later workers. As the Industrial Revolution progressed the invention of more advanced machinery began taking the cottage weaving into mill and factory conditions.

With the exception of forward thinking men such as David Dale and Robert Owen, who founded the New Lanark Mills, the conditions in most of these mills and factories were both hazardous and horrendous, with workers receiving little reward for the long hours and conditions in which they worked. The handloom weavers working from home were fearful for their livelihood and the cottage weavers in Motherwell decided to form their own friendly societies.

By the early 1800s Motherwell was on two much-improved main coach roads. The Turnpike Highway, which leads from Glasgow to Lanark, intersected with the second Turnpike Highway at Motherwell Cross, which lead from Hamilton to Edinburgh. The improvement of the road system gave a greater mobility to the area and stimulated growth. Along with the canal system already in operation, Scotland opened up. This, of course, had a much greater impact on the more remote regions but it certainly encouraged people to leave their areas, in most cases just looking for work. Motherwell was to become home to many people from other parts of Britain and indeed much later, in the world.

Archibald Hamilton of Dalzell was a very forward thinking man, aware of his status an influence in the community and genuinely concerned for his tenants and the land he had inherited from his ancestors. He wanted to see the land utilized to its best and for the benefit of all. Archibald Hamilton thus encouraged and welcomed individual tenant farming. The enticement he used was the granting of long leases, which in time would gave folk the chance to own their own land. Little could he have foreseen how his forward thinking schemes would be taken up by others, eventually creating 'Steelopolis.'

The records of the early Dalziel co-operative are somewhat vague and unfortunately a lot of their newer archived records had been destroyed in a flooded vault in Edinburgh. The first meeting to form a society in Motherwell took place on 10 November 1860. By the end of the first year they had seventy-three members with a capital of £196. The first shop was situated in Merry Street and the first few years were fraught with difficulties, but still the determined pioneers plodded on. In 1875 a man called Thomas Purdie joined the Society and it truly went from strength to strength. For close on sixty years this man guided it to great advancement. Men just as determined, such as A. Blair and A.K. Carruth, carried on the great work and the Dalziel Co-op became one of the biggest in Lanarkshire, with one of the highest dividend payouts.

The Co-op proved to be a great asset covering all basic human needs – food, clothing, footwear and medicine, and paid out a dividend to its members for their support. This dividend was often a boost to most families, especially amongst the working class.

Another factor and one of the most important for the industrial growth of Motherwell was the finding of the black diamonds – coal. The district was found to be abundant with rich coal seams, but it was not really until the middle of the nineteenth century that mining became more than a fledgling industry. I shall name a few pits now which I am sure will rekindle some memories: Parkhead, Broomside, Watsons, Coursington Camp, and Shields. The spin-offs from the mining industry were colossal, and iron companies amongst others, all added to the industrial boom that was Motherwell's. The steam engine and the coming of the railway proved to be the biggest bonus to the mining industry. Coal could now be transported anywhere as requested. The railway carried the coal and the coal fed the furnace.

The first railway line in Motherwell opened in 1841, connecting Motherwell and Coatbridge. The Caledonian Railway Company in 1848 opened up a new line, which connected Motherwell to the great city of Glasgow. The station was at Melville Road, while the present station in Muir Street was opened in 1885. The Jerviston Viaduct, known locally as the 'Globe Viaduct,' was built in 1840 and was the first viaduct in Scotland. It was used until 1857 and demolished in 1922.

The last and most crucial factor in Motherwell's industrial growth was Steel. The Steel story began with the vision of one man who is often referred to as the founding father of British Steel, David Colville, a shipping businessman who arrived in Motherwell in 1870 from Campbeltown on the Mull of Kinntyre.

In 1871 Colville bulit an iron works in Windmillhill. He was then feued land from the Duke of Hamilton, opening Dalziel Iron Works in 1872, which employed 200 workers. By the 1900s Colvilles had taken over the Clydebridge Steel and Glengamock Iron and Steel Company, and at the outbreak of the First World War they were the biggest steel producers in Britain. In the 1920s, with the boost of wartime production, Colvilles grow from a single steel works to a string of companies linked by rail throughout Scotland, merging with Stewart and Lloyds in 1934. The Second World War saw boom hit steel again, and Motherwell, with Colvilles Ltd, rolled more than nine million tonnes of steel. The 1950 Iron and Steel Bill lead to the establishment of the Iron and Steel Corporation of Great Britain and in 1953 the area was buzzing with the news of plans to build a steel city. It was to be called Ravenscraig, and to its workers it simply became known as 'the Craig'. A huge green-belt site, a mile south east of Dalziel Works was cleared, and on the 2 August 1957 the blast furnaces at Ravenscraig were lit. The plant at Ravenscraig was a visual landmark for years, while in 1967 Colvilles and thirteen other steel production companies passed into public ownership to become absorbed by the British Steel Corporation. In 1992 steelworkers at Ravenscraig were left reeling when British Steel said 'markets forces dictate a June closure for the plant', and finally, on the 27 June 1992, 1,220 steelworkers left the Craig for the last time. The blast furnaces were extinguished and Scottish steelmaking ended.

The heart is saddened to see the decimation of a once so powerful industry. There are now empty spaces where once there was a hive of industry with proud, hardworking men, but the spirit of the works and the steelworker lives on. The industry lives on in a different form in Dalziel Works, Motherwell Bridge and other names not operational now but still very close to the men who once served their time there, a proud legacy of 130 years of iron and steel history since a man called David Colville laid the foundation to create the Steel town.

Motherwell has a fairly mixed religious denomination as many settlers through the years came to make their home in Motherwell. Irish fleeing the potato famines, English, Scots, particularly from the highlands, and eventually people such as Poles and Lithuanians, who arrived to form a multicultural society. They have managed to live together in comparative harmony long since, counting themselves as Motherwell folk. Motherwell has its own cathedral and many beautiful churches, and long may they continue to thrive, prosper and flourish.

My husband Bill has often spoken to me about his boyhood days as a member of the Boys Brigade, as was his brother Peter. There were many Boys Brigade companies in Motherwell, each attached to a church. Bill was in the 5th company, attached to the Cairns church. His mother, whose maiden name was Galloway, and her family were members of this church, with brother Peter in the 13th company. Bill has spoken with happy and nostalgic reflection of his years in the Boys Brigade, from the junior to the senior section. One of his happy and proudest memories is when all the companies congregated at Thistle Street, packed full with boys and their parents and families. The Boys Brigade Drill Hall was there and all the companies in full smart regalia set off from Thistle Street to march proudly to the Duchess Park in Motherwell. It was a yearly event in which everyone took an active part, with proud parents and relatives looking on at these well groomed young men, each thinking their boy or boys the most handsome and smartest there!

Recreational pastimes in Motherwell have developed and progressed extremely well over the more recent decades. Recreation has always been part of the Scottish cultural scene and as a nation we have always done well in providing our own entertainment. Since the early records of our country and her people, entertainment within our societies such as families, clans, villages and towns has always been practised. For example, something just as simple as gathering around a fire with songs to be sung and stories to be told. Bonding such as this, especially for the working class families, was a form of escapism from the hard work and poverty, which was a part of everyday life. In later years, pastimes such as pigeon racing, dog racing, bowling, golf, tennis and swimming were to prove popular pastimes.

Motherwell has a number of public houses and social clubs where folk can meet for events and share time and companionship, while there is also a very modern Heritage Centre and an excellent and hard working historical society. The town has produced first class businessmen, born and brought up in the area and proud of their roots. The businesses long since established and respected include Skelly's, Brogans, and McPhaill's. William Struthers Moir Haulage was my husband Bill's family business. The family lived in Thistle Street in Motherwell and operated from Toll Street. The full name of the business was W.S. Moir and Sons, the sons at that time being Bill and Peter. The deliveries they made were quite far-reaching, with the Co-operative their biggest customer.

Motherwell is still thriving, albeit in what is certainly quite a difficult economic climate. How appropriate that the name of David Colville, although in a different spelling form, can be visibly seen in Motherwell to this day. I feel there is only one way to close this introduction – by saying what the supporters of Motherwell Football Club call almost every week: 'Come on the 'Well!'

One

A Walk Around Motherwell

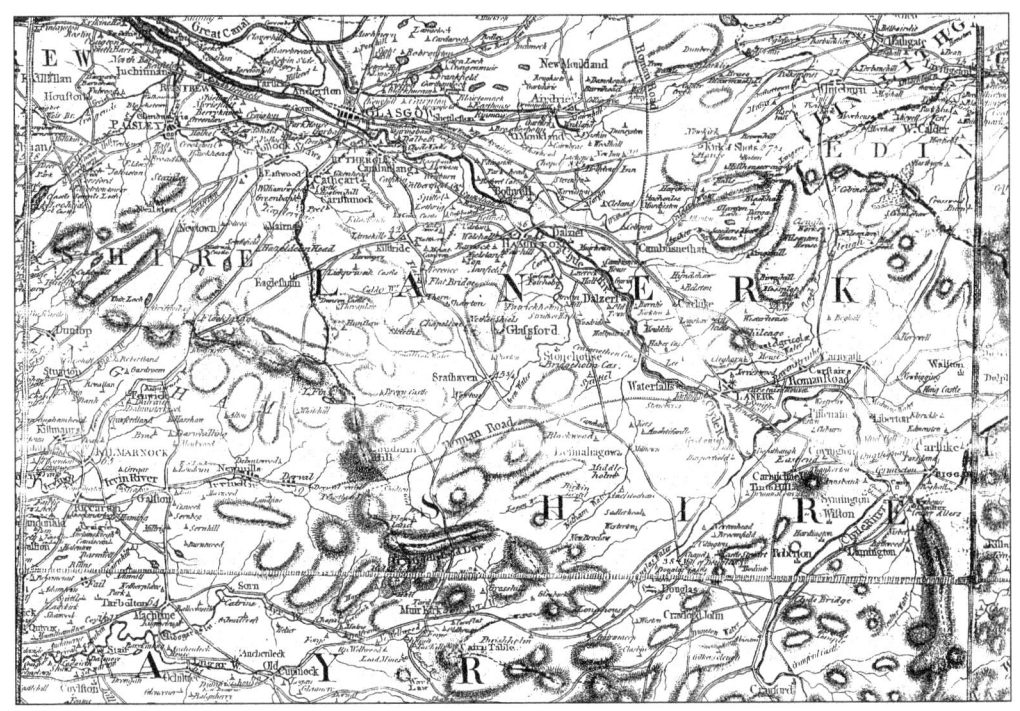

Map of Motherwell, 1789.

Motherwell Cross, c. 1950. This view shows Motherwell Cross looking down Hamilton Road. The traffic flowed a lot better then.

Looking up Brandon Street from the Cross. Dating from around 1910, this view shows the Cross before Brandon Parade was built. Wm Low's can be seen on the left.

Merry Street looking towards the Cross at the turn of the twentieth century.

Hamilton Road looking towards Hamilton, after the appearance of the trams.

Windmillhill Street in the 1950s. There isn't a bit of litter to be seen anywhere in this view.

Manse Road. At the time this view was taken, in around 1925, photographers were still very much a novelty and the children have willingly posed for this photograph.

Thistle Street no longer exists. The close knit community encouraged by tenement life meant that it was rare to come across a locked door and most people would look out for their neighbours and help. They created a real community spirit which is now lost in many parts.

An aerial view looking down on to Thistle Street. The small caravan that is visible belonged to my husband's parents and was christened the 'Wee Hoose' by their grandson, Billy Moir. Behind are the high rise towers which dominate this part of Motherwell now. The street running up the right is Airbles Street leading on to Airbles Road.

A 1900s view of Motherwell Cross taken from Brandon Street. The Cross seems to have been a favourite place to take a photograph, probably because it was the heart of the town and the most instantly recognisable part for many people. The people in this view are certainly aware that their picture is being taken.

A 1920s view of the Cross taken in Brandon Street. The Motherwell Inn is long demolished and Brandon Street has been turned into a modern, busy shopping precinct.

Mabel Street with some children out playing.

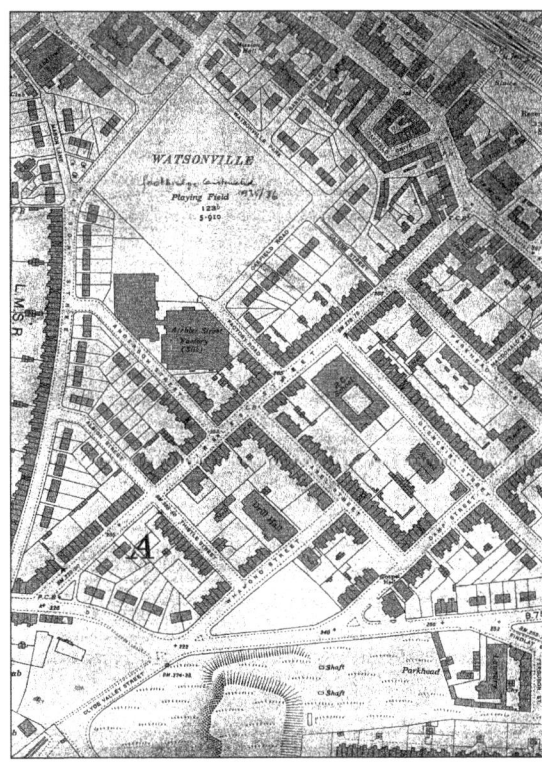

The 1939 Ordnance Survey map calls this street Mabel Street.

A view of Whammond Street in the 1920s showing the Drill Hall. Note the wee lad pushing the pram with the little lad following behind probably being his little brother.

Watson Street in the 1950s.

The present-day Clyde Bridge which connects Motherwell and Hamilton.

A view of the old Clyde Bridge, c.1910. This bridge was built in 1780 but the site of the bridge proved most unsuitable due to flooding in that part of the Clyde's route to the sea.

The remnants of the old Clyde Bridge. The bridge was built to plans by James Watt (of steam engine fame). Part was washed away in 1807 and on numerous occasions the bridge has been totally submerged.

Clyde Park, Motherwell, now part of Strathclyde Park.

Looking across the Clyde from Motherwell towards Hamilton. The building visible is the Hamilton Mausoleum built by Alexander, the 10th Duke of Hamilton, in 1846.

Trams came to Motherwell in 1903 and over 3,000 people used them on the first day of operation. This view shows two crossing the old Clyde Bridge.

This bridge is on the route of the old Roman road which passed through Motherwell. Although the bridge itself is not Roman it probably replaced a bridge of that era sometime in the sixteenth century.

Another view of the Roman bridge over the Calder. A legend says that Mary, Queen of Scots, moored her boat here when on a visit to Orbiston. An iron ring is still visible on the bridge.

Shields Glen, c.1910. The glen was bequeathed to the town by the Hamilton family and was officially opened in 1908 by Lord Gavin Hamilton. Today the glen suffers badly from vandalism and is now sadly in a very bad state of decay.

Another view of Shields Glen. I am sure that this place will hold many special memories especially for courting couples.

Dalzell House was once the seat of the Dalzell Hamiltons but has now been converted into luxury flats. The large spreading oak tree on the right is known as the Covenanter's Oak and it is said that conventicles were once held under its spreading branches.

Another view of Dalzell House. The Hamiltons of Dalzell can trace their ancestry back to the time of Kenneth McAlpine in AD 843.

The oldest part of Dalzell House is the Peel Tower which was built in the fifteenth century. Most of the house dates from the seventeenth and nineteenth centuries when it was greatly extended. The Hamilton family lived here till 1952 when the house became a school.

A view from Shields Glen. The high flats on Shields Road must have a fabulous view.

A 1938 view looking towards the Cross from Merry Street. Visible is Hamilton Road which was formerly called Clyde Street.

The old mill at Motherwell was owned for many generations by the McGregor family and it was often referred to as McGregor's Mill. The mill itself is one of the oldest in Lanarkshire and is now a hotel. It is often used for wedding functions.

Calder Park, Motherwell, 1938. The park was bequeathed to the town by Lord Hamilton in 1887 to commemorate the Golden Jubilee of Queen Victoria. At its industrial peak it must have been a blessing for many locals to be able to escape into these dens of tranquillity.

Jerviston House belonged to the Colville family in the 1920s. David Colville Junior, son of the founder of Colville's, lived here and after the end of the First World War the house was gifted to his workforce.

A view of the inside of Jerviston House. This gives an idea of the opulence to which the Colville family had aspired.

The old Jerviston Castle was also located on the Jerviston estate and has sadly been demolished. The castle was a typical Scottish Keep (or tower house) dating back to the sixteenth century and belonged to the famous Baillie family. A theory exists that the name Jerviston is derived from Gervase – a first name used and loved in the Baillie family.

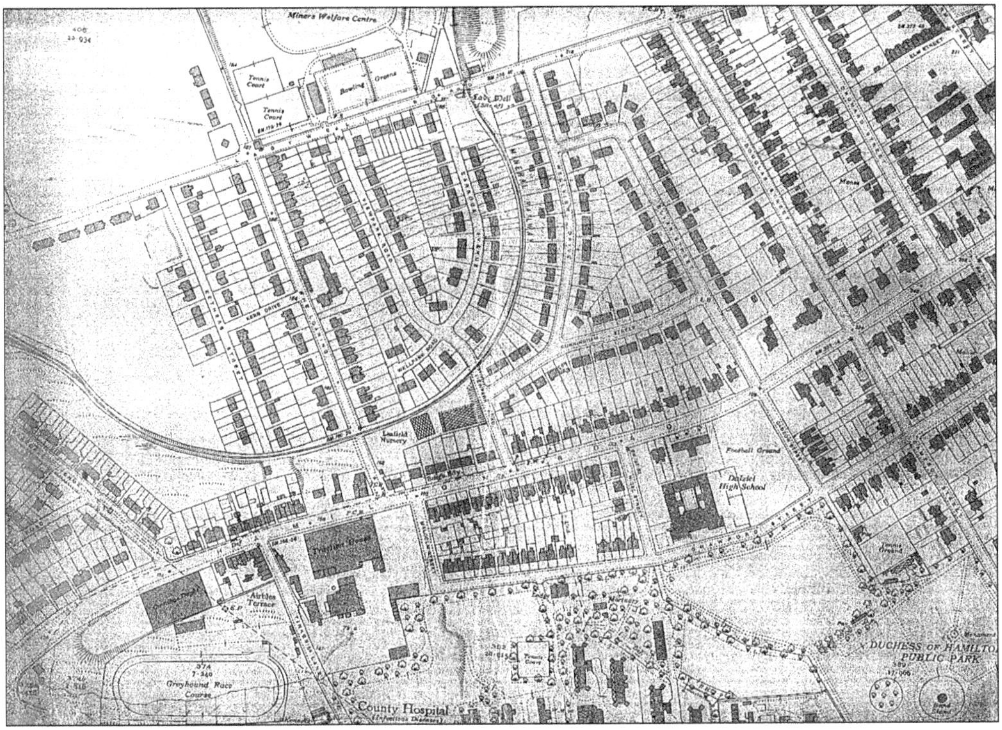

A survey map of Motherwell.

The Duchess park in the height of summer.

Carefree children have fun at the children's pool in the Duchess of Hamilton park.

The front of what was then the County Hospital. The 1939 Ordnance Survey map shows it as an infectious diseases hospital. My mother spent a few months here as a young girl suffering from rheumatic fever. The area is now Strathclyde Hospital.

The town hall in the 1930s. The building remains unchanged and was built in 1887 and opened by Lord Hamilton.

Motherwell's first town hall. The first town provost was Mr James Russell (1815-1911).

The insets of this view of the town hall are of James Russell and his successor, Mr Archibald.

Looking across from the North Church tower to the railway station and beyond. The High road and town hall are clearly visible in this 1930s view.

Hamilton Road. The end cottage belongs to Trixie Givens, the lawyer, who operates from the cottage. The cottage next door was a girls school in 1867. In 1830 it was occupied by one of the last weavers in Motherwell – an Alex Smith.

Looking up Brandon Street towards the Cross. This photo was taken in 1952. Just as you'd expect, three buses are coming along the street at once.

The Dalziel Co-operative buildings in Dalziel Street. Motherwell's first co-op opened in Merry Street in 1860. From that one little shop many followed including this one which is still in use by the Co-op today.

Dalziel High School is a fine building and was built in 1914 and opened in 1918. The standard of teaching was first class and the school has produced some notable pupils.

Dalzell House has now been converted into luxury flats and was once the home of the Dalzell Hamiltons. The house was built in the fifteenth century and was much extended during the seventeenth and eighteenth centuries. The family lived in the house until 1952 when it was converted into a boys' school until 1967. It lay empty for a few years and was then converted to its present use. Like many old houses it is reputed to be haunted.

Lord Gavin Hamilton of Dalzell.

A 1910 view of Flemington. The shopkeeper, with his white apron, would be able to watch the trams trundle past the door of his shop. Trams for all over Britain and the rest of the world were actually built in Motherwell.

Whistle Dry was a row of cottages which were mostly inhabited by weavers and tambourers. Its curious name comes from the fact that the builder of the row wouldn't allow his men to have a drink at the laying of the foundations. having a drink at the ceremony was traditional. A well-kent resident was the collier poet David Wingate. The van in the foreground belonged to Walter Gourlay who was a well known baker in the town for many years. These houses are long gone and the Rex Cinema resides on the site today.

Old Logan's is the name of this row of miners' cottages. Children play in the streets while their mothers watch from the doorways. This row was one of the first in Motherwell to have electricity.

The 1939 Ordnance Survey map. Much has changed in the town since this was published.

Wilson Street in the 1950s.

Another view of Jerviston Castle. It was sadly demolished in the 1970s.

Jerviston estate's lodge house.

The Delburn Falls. It is always amazing that such tranquil spots existed in the midst of so much heavy industry.

A view of late-Victorian Motherwell showing the town hall.

Motherwell Bowling Club is the oldest in the town and was founded in 1868. David Colville was made a life member in 1906.

Two

A Night at the Cinema

The La Scala cinema was located in Brandon Street. On the left hand side can be seen its cafe, also known as the La Scala.

The Cinema in Barrie Street. In the days before we all had televisions, the cinema was a major part of social life and you could go and watch the Pathé news, weekly serials like *Flash Gordon*, *Buck Rodgers* as well as stars like Myrna Loy, Jean Harlow and Greta Garbo.

The Odeon cinema has suffered the fate of many cinemas and has become a bingo hall.

This is the Pavilion which, like the Odeon, was situated in Brandon Street. Motherwell had a great choice of cinemas once and it is shame so many have disappeared. I am indebted to Scott McCutcheon for the selection. Scott is an avid collector of old and modern photographs of cinemas.

The Pavilion became the Majestic ballroom and continued as this until it was demolished.

Taken just after the beginning of the twentieth century, this view shows the New Century theatre in Windmillhill Street.

This lovely photograph of the Rex cinema is from the Lanarkshire Legacy Series and was taken by Mr J. McKillop. The 2,000 seater Rex was born out of the former New Century theatre. The cinema opened with with a screening of the Astaire/Rogers musical *Follow the Fleet* on 17 August 1936 and closed with a showing of the rather more controversial *Emmanuele* on 12 June 1976.

Three

Transport

Motherwell Cross looking from Clyde Street. A tram is sitting at the Cross. At one point you could go all the way from Motherwell, Hamilton or Larkhall to Balloch by tram if you were prepared to change and go on the Lanarkshire and Glasgow tram systems. Sitting on the open top deck on a nice day must have been great. Trams arrived in Motherwell in 1903.

A tram in Brandon Street, c.1910. As well as trams, the Lanarkshire Tramways Company also operated buses (mainly to those places it didn't serve by tram). By the late 1920s it was obvious that trams were expensive to operate – you needed so much costly infrastructure including rails, overhead electric wires and a power station whereas buses could be operated by a couple of people and go anywhere there was a road.

The real growth of bus travel came after the end of the First World War when so many people had learned to drive in the army and could afford to buy army surplus trucks and convert them. By 1930 it was obvious that the trams were in decline and the system shut shortly afterwards. This is another view of a tram in Flemington in the heyday of the trams.

The tramway power station was in Hamilton Road. The building still stands but has been converted to other uses. This photograph dates from 1904 and was published as a postcard by J.R. Ritchie of Edinburgh in their Reliable series.

An aerial view looking down onto Clyde Street, which is now Hamilton Road, Merry Street and the Cross. The tram has gone, the tracks are lifted and the bus has arrived. This photograph dates from the late 1940s.

This is a view of the Jerviston viaduct, built in 1840. It was also known as the Globe viaduct and below it was the Globe cemetery. The viaduct was demolished in 1922.

Another look at a tram in Hamilton Road. While the tram was often uncomfortable as it shoogled its was from terminus to terminus, the first buses that replaced it were often open and had solid rubber tyres. The speed of these first buses was only in the region of 12mph.

Motherwell's railway station is still a very busy place as this view can testify.

A Newmains-bound tram heads up Hamilton Road shortly before closure.

Local transport in the days before local companies like Skelly's were in existence. This is a Lanarkshire-registered steam bus from around 1905.

Ian Skelly of Skelly's Garage. Ian and his father have both been respected businessmen in the town.

Skelly's was an instantly recognisable landmark at the top of Airbles Road as this 1950s view can testify.

Crosshill Street, c.1928. This was the original Skelly's workshop and Joseph Mountney, seen here, was the first employee and grand uncle of Ian Skelly. He was a renowned pigeon fancier.

William G. Skelly, the founder of the original Skelly's.

The service team at Skelly's in the mid-1950s. The 1950s were a time of great change in the motor industry. There was an unprecedented growth in car ownership and British cars were a major force world-wide. Many names have disappeared since then including Triumph, Alvis, Riley, Wolseley, Morris and even Austin.

This was the site of the Clyde Alloy Steel Works, and is now the home of Ian Skelly's Motorstore, with lovely new premises.

Ian Skelly with his mother, c.1936.

Losing oil? Ian and Bill Skelly discuss the matter with Aberdeen expert, J. Faulds, at the Crimmond meeting in 1955. The car is an MG TF.

Four

Haulage

Brandon Street in the late 1940s. The man driving the horse and cart is my husband, Bill Moir, whose family owned the well-known haulage firm of W.S. Moir & Sons. Behind is the famous Brandon wall. The wee lad on the cart often enjoyed trips round town while Bill was delivering things.

Bill Moir outside his home in Thistle Street in the 1940s.

A line up of W.S Moir trucks in Thistle Street in the late forties. The gentleman standing beside the car on the left is William S. Moir senior, founder of the business.

Although the family lived in Thistle Street the business was operated out of Toll Street.

A 1966 view of the demolition of a house in Merry Street to make way for the new petrol station. Kelly & Sons are removing the rubble.

A Ford ET6 three ton truck delivered on 12 August 1953 to Ross, the local fruitier, by Skelly's.

One of Moir's Fordson trucks at Knowetop Avenue in the late 1940s.

Five

Industry

Ravenscraig Steel Works. Once a famous Motherwell landmark, 'The Craig' as it was known, employed a huge workforce of men from Motherwell and the surrounding area. On 27 June 1992, the final 1,220 steelworkers left Ravenscraig for the last time, its closure having a devastating knock-on effect to other businesses in the area. This excellent photograph was donated by James Muncie.

A trial erection of a bridge for the Ceylon Railway. Motherwell Bridge would often erect and test structures before they were shipped to their destinations world-wide. The top of the building peeking out above the bridge is St Andrew's parish church in Muir Street.

Taken in 1927, this view shows the staff of the No.2 Cogging Mill at Dalzell Works.

A 1920s view of Motherwell Bridge works when Motherwell Colliery was still in operation.

A 1909 view of some of the staff at Dalzell Steel Works. Do you recognize any of these hard working men?

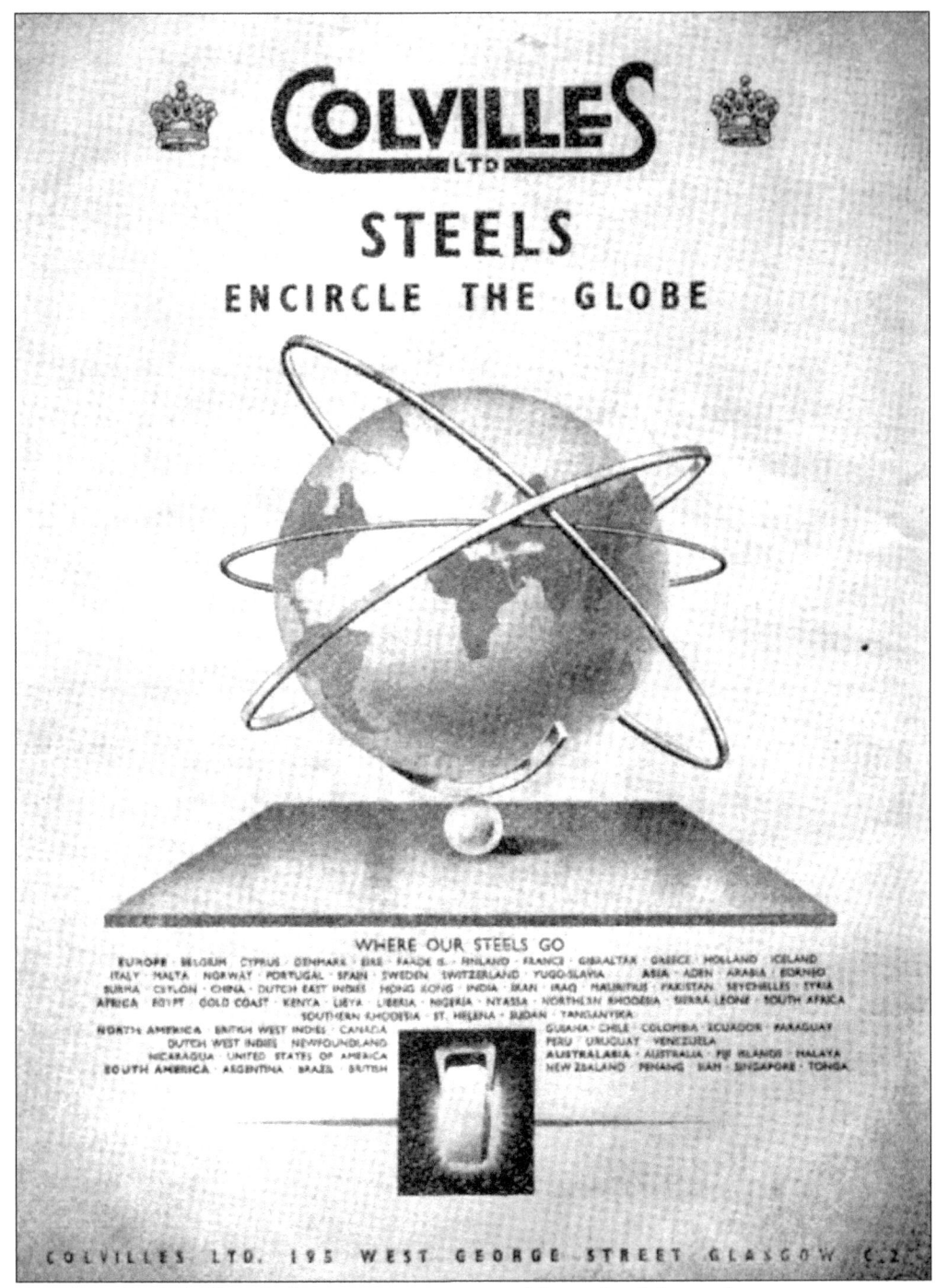

An advert for Colvilles which gives an impression of the scale of the works.

A group photograph taken in the pattern shop of the Lanarkshire Steel Company Ltd.

The white strips in this view of the inside of the Clyde Alloy Works are burning hot steel. This photograph was lent to me by Matt McCluckie of Ashgill who is the second man on the left working with the hot steel.

The triumphal arch built by Motherwell Bridge to commemorate the Coronation of Queen Elizabeth II in 1953. It stood on the Hamilton-Motherwell road near to the Clyde Bridge. In 1969 the structure was dismantled as corrosion had taken its toll on the arch.

Employees of the Motherwell Bridge Works in 1928. From left to right, back row; George Crichton – foreman engineer, William Coughtrie – foreman electrician, John Moffat – foreman marking shop. Front row, from left to right; John Jarvie – foreman driller, James Walker – foreman blacksmith, William Anderson – foreman fitting shop.

Employees of the Motherwell Bridge Works in 1928. From left to right, back row; John Anderson – foreman template loft, James Cowan – works manager, John Moffat – foreman marking shop, William Anderson – foreman fitting shop. Front row, left to right; John Jarvie – foreman driller, James Walker – foreman blacksmith, George Crichton – foreman engineer.

Mr Tom Shaw, of Larkhall gave me this view of the Motherwell Cleansing Department in 1933.

A view in Camp Colliery. This photo gives an idea of the horrendous conditions that many people had to work in.

Two miners ascending in the cage. The man on the left has lost part of his leg in a previous injury.

A 1933 view of the men of the heavy machine shop of Anderson & Boyes. At the front are the apprentices.

A 1977 photograph of Mr James Sykes collecting his award from the Rt Hon. Viscount Weir. Jim came third in the craft welding section in the Craft Trainee Competition Scotland Region 'Craftex 77'. He was representing Motherwell Bridge Engineering Ltd. Jim is a very experienced craft welder whose work has taken him abroad. He is now a grandfather.

The old Motherwell Mill.

Six
Churches

Dalziel parish church with an inset of its minister, the Revd G. Kerr McKay.

South Dalziel parish church.

St Mary's church. The inset photo is of the Revd William Smith BD. The Revd Smith was the first minister of St Mary's Parish. This 'Tin Kirk' was the second place of worship of St Mary's members whose church was then known as the Watsonville Mission of Dalziel parish church.

The interior of St Mary's as it is today.

The Kirk Session of St Mary's taken in May 1951. The minister sitting in the middle of the second row from the front is the Revd Ian Doyle.

The opening of St Mary's church garden fête in the church grounds at Cameron Street in 1950. The minister in the photograph is Ian, the father of the current minister, the Revd David Doyle. Mrs Margaret Barrowman, the Revd Ian Doyle, Mrs Anne Doyle, Jean Taylor-Smith the actress and Mr Alec Barrowman are facing the camera.

The presentation to Mr Angus Sutherland on his retiral from the position of church treasurer of St Mary's church in 1992. Mr Sutherland had been church treasurer for twenty-five years. He had also been manager of the Bank of Scotland in Motherwell. He is pictured in the front row with Revd David Doyle and Mr Howard Rennie, clerk to the Congregational Board. Also pictured are representatives of both board and session.

Carfin Grotto, Motherwell. The work of building Carfin Grotto began in 1920 under the guidance of Canon T. Taylor who had, earlier in the same year, gone on a pilgrimage to Lourdes with a group of his parishioners. They returned from Lourdes with a fixed project in mind to build a small replica of the Lourdes Grotto in Carfin.

The Little Flower Shrine at Carfin.

The Lourdes Shrine at Carfin. The grotto was dedicated on Sunday 1 October 1922 at the feast of Our Lady of the Rosary and the dedication was to Our Lady of Lourdes. Many miners on strike at the time volunteered to work on the building of the grotto.

John Bosco and Pious shrines.

Seven

Do You Recognize Anyone?

The Boys Brigade in the Duchess Park. Once a year all of the companies marched through the town to the park. They all met in Thistle Street and marched to the park with all of their proud relatives looking on.

The 13th Motherwell Boys Brigade Company of 1918/19. The Revd William Smith, first minister of St Mary's church, is pictured in the centre.

The 16th Company of the Motherwell Boys Brigade.

The 3rd Company of Motherwell Boys Brigade lead the rest through Motherwell, c.1910.

Taken outside the police barracks at the rear of Motherwell baths, this view shows St Mary's Guides in the mid-1920s.

St Mary's Guides marching down Avon Street in the mid-1920s.

Nan Rae, a famous Motherwell swimmer, being coached by David Crabb, the much renowned swimming coach.

The 1945 Motherwell Swimming Team is shown here. By this time the team held twenty-six records and had won thirty-three championships.

The mens team of Motherwell Amateur Swimming Water Polo Club. From left to right, back row; J. Cross, I. Johnstone, P. Gibson, J. Gibson, Archie Williams, E. Hope. Front row, from left to right; D. Jarvie, Forbes Gentleman, Bernard Brogan, D. Murray, J. Ferguson, Walter Houston, Jimmy Boyle.

An early photograph of Motherwell Town's Silver Band in their smart uniforms.

The award winning 1932 Dalzell Thistle Prize Pipe Band.

An early 1930s view of William S. Moir and his future wife Janet Galloway.

William S. Moir, his wife Janet and their two sons William and Peter in the mid-1930s.

This photogaph depicts five generations of William S. Moirs. Taken in the 1950s, it shows William S Moir sitting on the knee of his proud great-grandfather, William S Moir. On the right, standing, is the baby's father (shown as a child on the previous page), while the baby's grandfather (the William S. Moir of the previous page who married Janet Galloway) is shown standing on the left.

The latest in the line. This photograph shows William S. Moir being held lovingly by his sister, Nicole. The baby in the top photograph is now the proud father of these two children.

An early view of the Motherwell Salvation Army members.

The May Procession of 1914. The priest is Father O'Leary. I'm sure that few of the people here realised that only a few months later they would be involved in the First World War.

Taken inside the YMCA are soldiers being cared for by the Red Cross. So many men came back from the front injured that many large houses and halls were requisitioned to be used as VAD hospitals.

A group of people from the Gospel Hall out for an outing on the Beehive Brae in Flemington.

Mr and Mrs William G. Skelly with their 1953 Jowett Jupiter sports car. Jowetts were made in Bradford and the Jowett Jupiter model was a successful rally car and Le Mans racer.

Skelly's staff dance in 1955.

'The Big Man'. The late great Jock Stein, former Celtic and Scotland manager, who was a close personal friend of Ian Skelly.

Check out the prices. A local press advertisement for Skelly's from the early 1960s.

Jimmy and Nan Moir. For a long time Jimmy ran Moir Coaches in Motherwell.

These two happy couples are William S. Moir and Janet, his wife, along with Jock McPherson and his wife.

Colville Park Bowling Club in the 1950s.

The Ladies Opening at Colville Park Bowling Club in the 1950s.

These gentlemen are sampling the drinking water in the Duchess Park in the 1920s.

Taken at a Masonic dance in Motherwell, the people are from left to right: William S. Moir, Nessie Friel, Janet Moir, Jimmy Friel. Judging by the expressions on their faces, they were having a good time.

This family photograph shows, from left to right: Jessie Galloway, babe in arms Adam Galloway, Peter Galloway, Adam Galloway senior, Adam Galloway junior. The gentleman standing was sadly killed in a pit accident a few years later.

Mill workers outside the Old Mill in the 1940s. The man in the middle of this view of McGregor's Mill is William S. Moir.

Glencairn School pupils in the mid-1940s. Mr Wilson, the headmaster, is on the left.

Georgina Meekison, who hailed from Motherwell. Georgina married and became Georgina Moir. Shew worked for a time in the American Bar in Hamilton running it efficiently for John Skelton. She also helped run some of his other establishments.

A school photo from 1907. Mrs Perrie of Larkhall gave me this and her father, James McWhinnie Morton, appears in the front row, first left.

One of the early Motherwell fire brigades at Knowetop.

Eight
Football

Motherwell Football Club in 1899. The Lanarkshire Football League was started about this time and Motherwell FC was the first winner of this league.

John 'Sailor' Hunter's name is synonymous with Motherwell Football Club. He came in 1911 and became a renowned and well respected manager who took the team from strength to strength and who signed a few heroes of Scottish football.

Motherwell Football Club, *c.* 1895. The strip is much different from today's. (Charlie McBain kindly let me use these pictures of the 'Well'.)

Ian St. John of Motherwell, Liverpool and Scotland.

Motherwell won the Scottish League Cup in 1950. Captain Andy Paton is holding the cup and Willie Redpath the base. A proud moment for the town.

Motherwell in action against Falkirk. The score that day was 9-0 to Motherwell. On the radio the commentator could be heard saying 'Wee Pat Quinn scores again..'

This flower bed in the Duchess park was done to commemorate Motherwell's cup triumph in 1951/52.

The Ancell Babes Team.

The famous Bobby Ancell. When one talks about the Ancell Babes it is hard to forget the triumphs of the team against the best of Europe, the inauguration of floodlights, the sight of the Leeds keeper shaking his head in disbelief of his team's 7-0 drubbing and Bilbao being beaten 3-2 on a night when the heavens opened.

Motherwell's latest Cup success was the winning of the Scottish Cup in 1991. Here the team parade through town past the Cross in an open-top bus to let the fans see the Cup. Tom Boyd is proudly holding the cup.

Nine
Another Walk Around Motherwell

Motherwell Cross looking up to Brandon Street in 1939.

An aerial view of Motherwell.

Modern-day Motherwell Cross looking down to Brandon Parade.

The Cross from Merry Street.

Hamilton Road looking to the Cross.

Waiting outside Grafton's shop at the corner of Watson and Brandon Streets in the 1950s for the beginning of their sale.

This section of Brandon Street was widely referred to locally as 'The Brandon Wall'.

No.3 Dalziel Co-op at the corner of Brandon Street and Watson Street at the turn of the twentieth century. The bunting is to celebrate the Coronation of Edward VII and his wife, Queen Alexandra.

The copestone of the old Lady Well. The well dates from pre-Reformation times and was situated at the side of Ladywell Road on the Low Motherwell farm belonging to Robert Hamilton.

Mr Robert Hamilton at the site of the Lady Well.

Shields Glen is a beautiful place much loved and used by Motherwell folk.

Just look at those magnificent flower gardens. It must have taken a long time to care and tend the gardens at Shields Glen.

A. Torrance, Ltd.

★ ★ ★

DECORATORS AND PAINT MERCHANTS

★ ★ ★

173 Brandon Street, Motherwell

Telephone — Motherwell 134

Decorative Work of every description undertaken

Thomas Ross

Fruiterer and Florist

162 and 164 MERRY STREET
MOTHERWELL

Phone 1241

FRESH FRUIT and FLOWERS DAILY

WREATHS, SPRAYS and BRIDAL BOUQUETS made at shortest notice

On these pages and overleaf are a selection of adverts of local businesses. Do you remember the days of personal service and lots of assistants to look after you?

Alexander Fraser
(Bakers) Limited

HIGH CLASS BAKER
CONFECTIONER and
RESTAURANTEUR

Morning Coffees, Luncheons, and High Teas

Weddings and Social Functions of all kinds specially catered for

**35-39 MUIR STREET
MOTHERWELL**

Telephone: Motherwell 388

The finest things sold that's offered cold

Phone 710

"VERRECHIA"
All Cream   Ice Cream

Verrechia's Cafe at 11 Brandon Street has been completely re-equipped and redecorated throughout —why not pay us a visit?

VERRECHIA'S, 11 BRANDON STREET

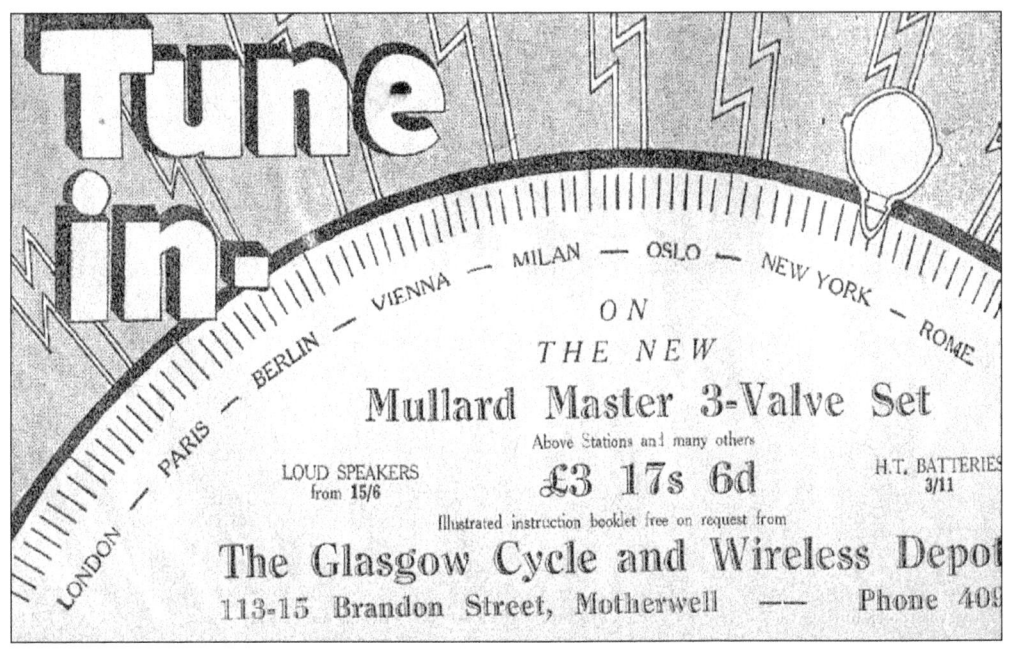

G.B. Russell grocers, a Motherwell shop of which the precise address is not known.

J. Gray & Sons, another of Motherwell's local family businesses.

Dundas Fyfe & Sons was established in 1878 and this photograph was taken in 1943 in Brandon Street. The family still provide a caring service today.

The funeral of the Revd Smith of St Mary's church in 1923. The old glass-windowed horse-drawn hearse belonged to Dundas Fyfe & Sons.

By 1933 Dundas Fyfe had acquired a motor hearse. This is the funeral of Councillor Ferguson.

A view of the premises of Dundas Fyfe & Sons.

People waiting for a function in the girl guide hall in Park Street.

The library in Hamilton Road.

The marvellous Motherwell Heritage Centre. The centre is run by very knowledgeable staff and holds a wealth of archive material and information. If this book has encouraged you to learn more about Motherwell's history I recommend a visit to here to find out more.

Motherwell Cross at the turn of the twentieth century.

Looking down Brandon Street from the Cross from the early part of the twentieth century.

A view of the old Police Office in Clyde Street. The first force numbered two people; Inspector Carmichael and a constable known locally as Larkie Bob because he came from Larkhall.

The Calder Bridge is in the background here in this view of the Calder park.

A more modern view of the Calder Park.

Another view of Dalzell House.

The Roman bridge which crosses the River Calder.

The old Clyde Bridge which was once on the main road from Motherwell to Hamilton.

Far removed from even the roads of the 1950s, this view is of the M74 and some of its fast moving traffic. In the distance is the skyline of modern Motherwell with its high rise flats.

Giving an idea of just how industrial Motherwell once was, this photograph was taken from Pollock Street looking towards Dalzell Steel Works. Today's council would have something to say about all of that smoke pouring out of the chimneys!

This is an old postcard as used by people to send to relatives all over the world. Before the telephone, postcards were used to keep in contact with all of your friends and relatives.

The old Clyde bridge can be seen in the distance in this early twentieth century view of the Clyde. This view has been taken from the Hamilton side of the river Avon.

Looking over to Hamilton from the Motherwell side of the river Clyde.

A multiview postcard used from the 1930s to the 1960s. The wee boy with the kilt appeared in postcards of places all over Scotland.

The new Motherwell Police Station. It is much different from the one shown earlier.

The new fire station in Delburn Street.

Extract from The Motherwell Times October 20th 1916.

PRISONERS RETURNED FROM GERMANY.

Private John Daly and Private Wm. French, 10th Gordon Highlanders, both Motherwell men, who were wounded and imprisoned by the Germans, have now returned to this country from hospital in Wesel.

Private French has been a prisoner of war in Germany for over a year. His brother Pte. Robert French, who was serving with The Argyle and Sutherland Highlanders, was killed about the time he himself was taken prisoner. The father of private French is in the service of Lord Hamilton of Dalzell, being lodge keeper at Clyde Bridge Lodge.

Pte Daly and Pte French, who were exchanged for German prisoners, are now lying in Queen Alexandra's Military Hospital, Millbank, London.

A sad, but self-explanatory, extract from the Motherwell Times of 16 October 1916.

Extracts from the Motherwell Times November 3rd. 1916.

RETURNED FROM GERMANY – LOCAL LADS' EXPERIENCE.

Among the disabled soldiers returned by Germany is Pte. John Daly, Gordon Highlanders, who is presently an inmate of a military hospital in London. Pte. Daly's home address is in Kirk Street.

Another Motherwell lad, Pte. William French, Gordon Highlanders, is also in the same hospital. Pte. French's father is lodge keeper at Clyde Bridge.

Pte. Daly, who is 19 years of age, was employed at Dixon's Colliery, Carfin. he was wounded at Loos in September last year, was captured by the Germans, and placed in hospital, where it was found necessary to amputate one of his legs. Three other brothers also joined the army. One was killed at Mons, another has been discharged wounded, and the other is in hospital in Salonica.

Private French, who has also lost one of his legs, was taken prisoner at the battle of Loos. He is the only one left of three brothers who joined the army. One of them was killed in action, and the other died of wounds in a German hospital.

Both of these Motherwell lads were in the same German hospital at Wesel, and are now companions in the London hospital, under happier conditions.

HOSPITAL OF HORROR.

Private William French had a remarkable story to tell to a "Sunday Post" representative regarding the inhumanity of the surgeons in German prison camps.

Private French says that he might have had his right leg yet had the German doctors been human. At the hospital at Wesel the doctors were nothing better than students, who were only there to gain experience.

He refused to have his limb amputated, but the doctor insisted, and after taking off the limb told the prisoner that his was only the second limb he had amputated. The doctor was a veritable butcher, and many other prisoners who had to undergo an operation at his hands had not survived, whilst even the German wounded objected to his treatment.

After Pte. French left the hospital of horror he was sent to the camp at Friedricksfeldt.

"Things", he said, "were pretty bad when I went there first, but I'm thankful to say that the treatment has improved considerably, and is likely to do so as long as our men keep going forward in France.

I'm glad to think the conditions have changed.

Think of it – in the winter of 1915 some of our lads were pegged down in the snow for refusing to work. For the same reason men have been tied to trees with their feet off the ground, and left in that position for hours at a stretch."

Private French makes light of his own troubles. Very soon he expects to be transferred to Paisley, where he will get an artificial limb and once again he will see the "auld folks at hame".

An article from the Motherwell Times of 3 November 1916. These extracts were given by Mr Robert French.

The Civic Centre has seen much change in its short life. Motherwell District Council has given way to North Lanarkshire Council but the Civic Centre is still a hive of commerce, entertainment and local government.

The Aquatec – one of the modern buildings springing up in Motherwell. The town has always been renowned for its champion swimmers.

The Aquatec again.

This grand old building is the Cathedral – a well known Motherwell landmark.

Another view of the cathedral.

The Civic Centre.

My husband, Bill Moir, doing his National Service in the Royal Air Force. Like many, he was conscripted for two years. Some were lucky and saw service in places like Germany while others went to Cyprus and Malaya to fight rebels, or were sent to Christmas Island to take part in atomic bomb tests.

Attending a local function are, from left to right: William S. Moir, Janet Moir, Mrs Calder and her husband Alex Calder, manager of the Dalziel Co-operative bakery in Motherwell.

Anderson and Boyes Company Limited, Light Machine Shop, 1927. Motherwell folk have every right to be proud of their industrial background. What a heritage! What a legacy!